The World Within

The World Within

Poems
by
Ellen Murphy, CSJ

Without the world within, no world without . . .

Illustrations are reproduced from "Creation"
an original embroidery made in 1997 by Baya Clare, CSJ

ISBN: 0-87839-303-X
ISBN13: 978-0-87839-303-9

Printed in the United States of America.

Published by North Star Press of St. Cloud, Inc
PO Box 451
St. Cloud, MN 56302
www.northstarpress.com

Foreword

"Without the world within, no world without." These words from Ellen Murphy's poem, "To Stop the Rose," capture a self-description of Ellen's poetry and of Ellen herself. The poems published in this collection represent nearly sixty years of her appreciation of beauty and her deepening growth in wisdom. Ellen Murphy in her lifetime wrote over 200 poems from the 1930s (or before) to the 1990s.

Ellen Murphy's rich and gentle life extended over eighty-eight years, from 1916 until 2004. From the time she could hold a pencil until old age (when her final poems must have remained unspoken in her consciousness) she lived, loved, and wrote poetry, usually under her given name but for a time under her religious name, Sister Agnes.

Sister Ellen came from a literary family. From earliest childhood, she wrote stories and poems, including daily letters to her family when she was away at boarding school. In junior-high school, she received the gift of a journal from her mother, herself a keeper of journals. Ellen began to keep her own journal and was faithful to it until her final illness many decades later. From her mother, Ellen learned independence, courage, and determination: qualities found in many of the poems focusing on her family and her early life. She inherited from her father his Irish wit and gentle compassion.

Young Ellen, who became Sister Agnes when she joined the Sisters of St. Joseph in 1935, wrote the poem "Their Father" in the autumn of 1944. This poem won the Catholic School Press Association prize in 1945. For this young woman who became a metaphysical poet herself, the prize foreshadowed the direction her poetry would take.

This prize, *Poems of Gerard Manley Hopkins*, was edited with notes by Robert Bridges, poet laureate of England, who had brought to light the great metaphysical poetry of Hopkins in 1918 (Critical edition by Charles Williams, Oxford University Press, 1944). Sister Ellen's poetry reflects the life she knew: a profound sense of what it meant to belong, to be loved, to have a permanent place in her universe. Her sensitive heart was vulnerable to overwhelming loneliness whenever she was separated from her beloved family. However, her charm and wit won her many friends wherever she went.

Her gift of poetry grew with her life experiences. She wrote nearly every day of her life, poetry becoming a habit and a virtue. A colleague, in praising her poetry, told her she had "the virtue of poetry." Her poems, especially the later ones, revealed to her friends and colleagues a sparkling wit and lightness that accompanied the depth of her insights.

Since Sister Ellen's death in 2004, her poems have rested like rare jewels in the treasury of the archives of the Sisters of St. Joseph, St. Paul. Now we open them to the light to share them as they deserve to be shared. Ellen's poems, in their simplicity, their vivid imagery, and their fresh view of life are not unlike the poems of Emily Dickinson also found after her death.

And like the metaphysical poetry of Gerard Manley Hopkins, her large body of poetry expresses deep thought in imagery which is transparent but profound, simple but deep. Sister Ellen also sensed the greatness of the scientist/theologian/poet Teilhard de Chardin, who was also aware of the luminosity of God glowing within nature.

We have selected fewer than 100 of Ellen's poems and present them here in the order in which they were written (as far as we are able to determine). The table of contents follows the order of the decades of composition from the thirties to the nineties. A line from a poem of the decade opens each section.

The title of the collection, *The World Within*, we have chosen from her poem "To Stop the Rose" (written in 1967). Its first line captures the essence of all her poetry: "Without the world within, no world without . . ."

Editors

Eleanor Lincoln, CSJ, and Catherine Litecky, CSJ, Professors Emeritae
The College of St. Catherine, St. Paul, Minnesota
Currently Co-directors of Women at the Well Ministry,
St. Paul, Minnesota

A Reflection on
Ellen Murphy's Life

Ellen Murphy's poetry is still virtually unknown, yet she deserves to be recognized as a writer who had come to know deep secrets of existence. She named a collection of her poetry *Body of Time*, to express her views of what can be seen and measured, from the simple to the sublime, as compared to worlds beyond. She expressed her felt world with glimpses of worlds that harmonized with the natural. She believed, as did Keats, that "I am certain of nothing but the holiness of the heart's affections and the truth of the imagination." She was accurately named a metaphysical poet for the epiphanies which she expressed.

As a young girl growing up on the flat plains of Eastern North Dakota, she referred to herself as Ellen of the Prairie for, she said, the "land with its endless horizons, space, and solitude were inspiration for the poet in me."

Born in 1916, the child of prairie pioneers, on a farm some miles north of Grand Forks, North Dakota, she was a second and shy child. "Shy until I die," she said. Ellen and her siblings went to one-room country schools or boarding schools for primary education. Very often they braved heavy snowstorms in order to get to their classes, driven by trusted horses who always knew the way. The world of the farm in the 1920s and 1930s was harsh and demanding yet her loving, creative family developed in her a depth for sweet appreciation and wonder for the natural world. Farm life and an uncertain livelihood, because of the exigencies of weather and markets, made the Murphy family life difficult. Acceptance of life and all its struggles led her to conjure up an interior life where she found solace and some certainty.

Leaving the farm in 1931, as the Depression years deepened, to board at St. James Academy in Grand Forks, was a wrenching experience for her. Because her beloved French mother and her dear Irish father held education in such high regard, nothing seemed to prevent the four Murphy children from getting to the best schools. Their lives revolved around the cattle, the crops, and schooling.

Living forty miles away from home in a convent high school gave Ellen the inspiration, the aspiration, and the courage to pursue a religious vocation. In 1934 she entered the religious order of the Sisters of St. Joseph in St. Paul, Minnesota. She may have desired, as Gerard Manley Hopkins, another metaphysical poet, wrote in his ode to a nun taking her vows:

> *I have desired to go*
> *Where springs not fail,*
> *To fields where flies no sharp and sided hail*
> *And a few lilies blow.*
> *And I have asked to be where no storms come . . .*

The order gave her an excellent education with an emphasis on literature. She received an undergraduate degree from the College of St. Catherine and later a graduate degree from the University of Notre Dame.

She began her professional life as a teacher of the very young. Hundreds of children were given a wise and loving introduction to the life of the mind and soul because of her dedication to them. The final years of her career she spent at the College of St. Catherine as a professor of education and also shared her love of poetry in creative writing sessions. She was specially trained to teach Maria Montessori's educational methods to the students. Those years were a time of intense work for a woman who then might well have ended her teaching career and retired to the quieter life of a poet. Her mettle in many ways was tested. She even had to learn to drive a car in order to supervise her students.

Ellen said that "lonesomeness is part of my life." Yet here was no lonely spirit, but that very trait gave her the need to plumb the depths of her poetic self. Ellen's work life in teaching was her first occupation but she stole moments, and then hours and days, to write her poems. For more than seventy years she wrote in praise of the natural world and its relationship to the supernatural. She transcended the ordinary world to which she was so obedient for the glory of another world most real to her. In 1994 she wrote:

We're evanescences
eternalized
in spirit though
the body dies
on earth, our star, and we remain
most eloquently who we are.

From her description of a vivid rainbow, roses, or pomegranate seeds, to sophisticated references to theories of suspended time and quantum physics, she wrote quietly and modestly while living out her vocation: her promise to serve God. Her religious vows allowed a distillation of her soul thoughts into poetry. She was penetrating the mysteries of other worlds via her regard for the created universe, influenced deeply by her North Dakota heritage.

Ellen died in 2004 at Bethany Convent in St. Paul at age eighty-seven, taking with her promises of better worlds to come because of the life she wrote of and lived so very well.

Sandra Murphy, niece,
November 7, 2007

In Gratitude

Many people have made the publication of these poems possible. We are grateful for their encouragement, support, and helpful suggestions. These include:

Mary Kraft, CSJ, archivist of the Sisters of St. Joseph, supported us in uncovering the material stored in the archives and gave us encouragement throughout.

Sandra Murphy, Ellen's niece, has uncovered some Murphy family material and made it available to us. She has supported and encouraged us from the beginning. Her close relationship with Ellen is evident in her loving reflection on her.

Baya Clare, CSJ, computer expert and artist, has helped us in innumerable ways, including her designs for the cover and the sectional pages.

Mary Lou Matt, CSJ, Ellen's personal friend, provided us with the floppy disc that contained all of Ellen's two hundred plus poems, and she has helped us through her constant encouragement.

Ann Thompson and Jan Zitnick, in the Sisters of St. Joseph of Carondelet Communications Department, have graciously helped us in a number of ways, including the layout and design of this book.

Carolyn Puccio, CSJ, member of the CSJ provincial leadership team, supported from the beginning our endeavor to bring Ellen's poems to light and saw to their publication.

And the many others who have supported and encouraged us in this project.

Gratefully,
Eleanor Lincoln, CSJ, and Catherine Litecky, CSJ

The World Within

Poems

by

Ellen Murphy, CSJ

Without the world within, no world without . . .

Part 1

Poems of the 1930s/1940s/l950s: "Wisdom will begin like this" (from *Beginning of Wisdom, 1947*).

Part 2

Poems of the 1960s: "What you hear is the heart sound"
(from *What You Hear*, 1960).

Part 3

Poems of the 1970s: "A way of seeing shapes a way of being" (from *Preference*, 1975)

Part 4

Poems of the 1980s: "Our earth explains our God"
(from *Three Acts of Love*, 1986).

Part 5

Poems of the 1990s: "We're evanescences eternalized in Spirit" (from *Evanescence*, 1994).

Part 1
Poems of the 1930s, 1940s & 1950s

"Wisdom will begin like this"
—from *Beginning of Wisdom*, 1947

Cherry Blossom Heart

A gentle, aged woman,

Why do you hoe those potatoes?

You are so lovely

In your white frilled apron

and starched bonnet

I know you have

A cherry blossom heart.

> Found in *The Wild Rose*, a quarterly publication of
> Academy of St. James, Grand Forks, North Dakota,
> Spring 1932.

Two Poems

I.

Just a thin white covering
With soft black mud showing through,
And a green cart rumbling
O'er the March road—while the wind blew.

II.

Under a simple and sheer-blue sky
We walk together—she and I;
She gathers the ferns and the daisies sweet,
I gather the blue flowers in the wheat.

Found in *The Wild Rose*, a quarterly publication of
Academy of St. James, Grand Forks, North Dakota,
Spring 1932.

On All Saints Day to My Friends

O blessed who possess the land
and lead me as the light leads in the wide
and quiet sky; as branches lead the eye
freely, and reaching lovely up and out
signalling with green leaves and golden sun
until I look and come.
                              I look and come.
And straight through the clear colors of your love,
complete and single in the splendid sky,
I find the center where the light is white.
I look and love, desiring to become
O . . . nothing less than blessed. And to be
forever loved in this simplicity.

1943.

Their Father

Their father always went out in late April
or early May to plant the warming land
with seeds stored from last year. It was as certain
as sunrise he would go, his pipe in hand.

His grey eyes took account of the spring weather
the while he hitched his horses to the drill.
He would go riding, whistling over the furrows—
up and down through all his fields until

his land was full of promise. Through the summer
he would watch, anxious as a mother does,
the growth of the young wheat. O, he was careful
not to count too much on it, for he was

a farmer's son. He knew the odds of farming.
He had seen drought, and grasshoppers, and rust.
But he was God's son also. He could whistle
come blight or hail. He knew Whom he could trust.

1944.
Awarded Catholic School
Press Association prize, 1945.

The Children and the Mourning Doves

They had nothing in their young hearts to answer
The deep, sad calling of the mourning doves
From cottonwoods and granary. Their calling
Was strange to all the bright and moving loves

The children knew. Yet they had seen their mother
Look from her work to listen. They could see
She loved the song of doves. There was such stillness
Came to her eyes when they called . . . as if she

Knew something very beautiful and lonely;
Something too great and sad and far away
To tell her little children. O, they wondered
How she could listen to the doves while they

Answered the shrill insistence of the blackbirds,
And sang with robin and with meadowlark.
They were not schooled yet to the tune of sorrow.
They feared the doves' call as they feared the dark.

1945.

Beginning of Wisdom

Wisdom will begin like this
when sharp, clean winds of holy fear
sweep the curved roads of our good will
bringing to light the deep ruts and the stones.

All through the leafless hedges of our minds
this wind will whip like a stern prophet's voice
and we will listen, taut with our own hurt,
and rake the lawn and burn the dry, dead leaves.

Then come like rain, O lovely Piety,
drop from the April clouds of our compunction
bringing new grass and violets and lilacs.

Fair love will come to May-time while we say our prayers.

And on the gold-green branches
the seven gifts will flower in the Sun.

Come, O clean wind of Holy fear,
for water and the Holy Ghost have marked
these narrow acres for an endless spring.

1947.

Lines upon Returning

We came away then at the right moment
Leaving our country somewhat as they leave
Who go to war. (For we had gone to war;
All down the road our hearts were fiercely riddled
By the remembered eyes at the lonely door.)

We pulled away from the green willow branches,
Ran through the barricades of golden barley,
Broke through the rooted things where our hearts had grown
Quietly in the sun; where all that our eyes saw
Had been there always the same and always our own.

Because they pointed with brown hands to the rainbow
And to the new moon over the cupola, directing
Our eyes to this high beauty, we had to go
Away from the arms that held us, the lips that told
Of the sun and stars of another land that we did not know.

We had to take a running start to reach this mountain,
Sending the mind ahead where the heart couldn't follow
Being not quite broken free from the lilac bush in the yard
And the waving hands that brushed the eyes that smiled
As we ran alone to the mountain that was so hard.

Oh, it was hard to the feet and beautiful to climb
With nothing to cling to and the sunlight blinding
Or night pitch black when the unminded tears
fell in the strange land until we found the place
Where the hands had pointed in the long, light years.

We found it in time upon the timeless mountain:
The promise of the rainbow and the sun's bright glory
So that we can return and clasp the rough, brown hands
And smile into the eyes that watched us go away
And find in them the beauty of these high, bright lands.

1948.

The Image

This hardness guards the seeds of spring . . .
such is the winter of our love.
The stiff dark trees will someday bend
their green-skinned branches to the birds.

The bare earth carries future flowers
darkly under a frozen breast.
Such is our love's cold desolation
because all birth resembles death.

And we who wait the south-wind's season,
humbled with coldness under the cloud,
know when the shroud of love is loosened
heaven and earth will sing aloud . . .

Wings in the leaves, and blue-bells ringing . . .
how to tell what the spirit brings?
Out of the hardness of love
the barren flowers, the fountain springs.

1950.

The Blessed Virgin Mary's Assumption

It was the Sun that drew her up from the earth
as lilies lift at His light, as daisies rise
fresh as the morning out of the dark ground,
as iris open to flower in His eyes.

It was the Sun whose light lay curled so long
under the folded petals of this Rose
that now drew her with strong, invisible fingers
up from the grassy mound of her repose.

It was the Sun took root and leaf and petal
straight into Heaven where no other grew;
drawing her wholly by His radiant longing
simply as sunlight lifting the morning dew.

1950.

The Pearl

The kingdom of heaven is like a priceless pearl
hid in the deep sea's heart
under the green, the cold grey waters,
under the rock and the tangled weeds.

Love will discover the priceless pearl, no other.

It is nowhere in space unless you go there with closed eyes
under a grassy mound, under banked snow,
your bones in the ground. (Then you have found the pearl)

Space is a place for skies, for wide trees,
These and a time to die. But the pearl lies
where the Spirit moves unseen in the rich waters. (the pearl
that is locked, precious, in our flesh
since we came from the sea of our nativity)

Sell all the life you love for it.
And when you dive in death, breathless,
through rock and weeds, through tangles of green and grey
on the way from time and space. That night
you will arise in day and find the pearl,
the whole round pearl of heaven.

1950.

13

We are not now, but we shall be . . .

Our phoenix future kindles from green ashes.
Flame that we are not folds a crystal fire
until our absence glows in the charred hollow
and fills with light the bright plumes of desire.

We are not now. Beneath a wing of smoke
the grey heart smoulders, molten veins go blue.
Our cycle curves a wider arc than fire.
The pyre cradles us and we are new.

Shall be! O winning Wind, though we are not
This flame of longing in the phoenix breast
shall break the seeming seal of the horizon
and lift the still wings to their radiant nest.

1951.

14

Annunciation

Wind of the south, our green-winged Gabriel comes
Visible in the virgin light of dawn
kneeling in wonder among bridal branches,
bearing consent from lilac tree and lawn.

Date from his shadow what the questioning sun
begins in snow at the first yes of spring.
This is the secret beautiful incarnation
of every stem from which the blue-bells ring.

The flowering breath of the annunciation
moves through our minds. The weather of our will
works with the sun and wind in their creation.
Hope fills our veins like some bright chlorophyll

Coloring all our love with the sun's power.
What grew so pale in climates of deep night
lifts in this light as lovely as salvation
Where Gabriel, our south wind, knelt in flight.

1952.

Your Grief Will Be Turned into Joy

Psalm 125 (126)

Grief-stricken, you pause to wonder how this will be.
Eternal joy the sum of time's dark cumulative sorrow?
Lifelong pain to bring surcease from pain? You've learned to know
the inner tensions art and prayer resolve. Mozart, head bowed
in reverence for his heavy heart composed from time on earth
the sacred sound of grief turned into joy.
Beethoven storming in and out of love and growing deaf
to earth's heart-stirring sounds composed from this
his lofty Ninth, the symphony profound
that ends with a triumphant Ode to Joy.
It must be so. On lower planes you feel
the poem-trauma of a songbird felled. You see from crippling age
the broken branches of a blossoming tree. Wild clover seared with sun,
its bloom, its fragrance gone. The delicate, clean skeletons of those
enchanting small wild creatures of the woods
hunted, bereft of life. Tall, shielding grasses crushed.
All dust. The withered petals in the flower bed. Summer's bequest
a compost rich with darkest death. You've seen what comes of this.
Earth's revelations lighting up
the grounds for grief in every temporal loss: homestead, hayfield,
dooryard, wheatfield, fences, meadowlarks.

The sparrows on the weathered window-ledge
coming and going like the mood for joy. An evanescence there
reminding you that loneliness is love. That no one—nothing you
have ever loved will die. That home's old floorboards once again
will sing as when, nimble and light you slipped
upstairs and down in dreams within
the longed-for then and always. The ripe garden scene:
networks of berry bushes, clover, grass. The yield
of leaf and petal rhyme, lilac, wild roses, white anemone.
Rhythms of time and weather, the crisp ring of crystal frost
and snow. Its beauty. Its white light and its cold sting.
You walk in time that hurries you away. No one can stop
the darkness falling as it measures light. The two are one—
a lonely comfort as you count each friend
whose life-sustaining life will one day seem to end. Leave violets
untended, hymns and songs unsung. That one
quick with old melodies and the apt quote
that deepened and extended what was said
in taking life to heart, in being there—in letting go . . .
Muse, mentor, friend.

1952.

A Tree Has Hope . . . Job: 14:7

On observing the broken bough of an oak tree
from a hospital yard on Good Friday.

Our eyes were lifted to the vacant lot
across the way. The top branch of an oak
was cut abruptly off. A leafless black bough caught
our glances where it broke the sky. One stroke
had left it stiff as death though all the rest
tossed greening buds from roots the spring had touched.

I thought of continuity and blessed
the moment's meaning when I heard you bring
brave sanction to the sight. With Job you said,
"A tree has hope." Then we walked on among
the gold-skinned willows; saw the seeming dead
catalpa stir, its grey boughs growing young,
unfolding tight, white flowers. You and I
turned to the hospital. Our April tour
had cleared the weather of my clouded sky.

"It groweth green again . . ." All hope stems sure
from sacred boughs upstretched. A red-veined tree
bears out Job's promise—immortality.

1959.

For Pere Teilhard de Chardin at My Father's Grave

1. Not long ago his children's children skimmed
an all saints' sky and via leafless boughs
they brought down twenty empty nests or more.
We watched indoors while he, with laboring breath,
climbed motionless inviolable skies.
Through rigid winter mourning tears matured
the roots of vision rising through the heart
until we knew that loneliness is love
unseen and hope the very bone of earth.
In cemeteries larks are singing life.
I meditate the winter's skeleton
limber again with the light touch of spring
and think of you, Pere Teilhard de Chardin,
scholar of bones, in your changement d'etat.
It is memorial day among these stones
and ceremony serves my heart. I lay
today's limp lilacs on the granite name
and look toward doom's day for his gentle face.

2. My father's death unwinters with the trees.

Through the tradition of his pulse and breath

he moves the prairies towards his total home

where Christ extending brings a realm of dust,

his skull, the site of science and belief,

his ribs, the residence of love's insights,

into intelligence of timeless may.

I see his life in the pleroma lift

from eye-sockets and breast-bones, bowls that held

particular plumb worlds, his every-day

etudes perduring through old finger-bones:

poetry, politics, a garden fence,

persons affirmed, a branch diaphanous

with blackbirds singing in a cottonwood.

1959.

Published in *Commonweal*, January 22, 1960, p. 194,

and in *Body of Time*, 1971.

Part 2
Poems of the 1960s

"What you hear is the heart sound."
— from *What You Hear*, 1960

Elegy

The mother answered, "It is true. I know.

This ancient apple-tree is past bearing
but it blooms in my mind. I shall not let
them cut it down. Its yield in love preserves
incalculable sweets, the apple years.

It is two-thirds memory, holding the spring-
time nests, the song. And I am old, feeding
birds in the barren branches where the cats
prey fruitlessly among the stirring shadows.

Sometimes my son returns to muse among
the boughs. I've seen him look up absently
and mark two old grey branches with his eyes
reverent against the day of the uprooting.

Some thought of his lives in this apple-tree;
a poetry of the past that is his only.
For though he is young we become in our
different ways lonely, keeping what we can.

Here the duress of dying eases for
me. The strain of age is buttressed by this
beautiful structure of what has been. It
leans in the yard, my dark-leaved apple-tree."

1960.
Published in *Commonweal*, January 8, 1960 and
in *Body of Time*, 1971.

Dusk

A minor miracle occurred tonight.
A rusted rake turned up the scent of green
along the lily-of-the-valley bed
just as a blackbird with a red wing spread
whirred through the dusk, half heard and half unseen.

This moment of indefinite delight
reminded me of somewhere out of mind
I could not place with bridal wreathe nor plum
nor branch where high-flown cardinals had come.
My eyes closed on a face I could not find.

Then the lids parted. Lonely second-sight
struck a brief light to show me where you are.
The rake was put away. The loam, the nest
blurred in the dusk. Their rest and my unrest
stirred the new darkness at the first dim star.

1961.

A Nun Remembers Her Bridal Day

Remembering, as brides of years will do,
I see the laundry tubs where roses kept
the day before our wedding. Light was bleak;
a typical March day. I hear the creak
of rubber ice when, lightly though I stept,
deep ruts cast silver splinters at my shoe.
There were wide puddles where the clothesline stood.
Part of my trousseau shimmered in the sky
that shimmered in the water where it hung.
I could not reach it, being small and young,
and had to ask a taller passer-by.
My hair blew soft and brown. It felt so good
floating upon the breeze. Tomorrow's veil,
My floating hair shorn! Freedom! Skimming feet!
My very thoughts would stiffen and go dry.
I had not chosen Him. He heard me sigh.
The wedding was tomorrow. I must greet
His Love with love. That Love had made me pale.
Fearing decorum, discipline's stern walk
through the dry places of the lands He gave—
what would he make of me? Some stiff, dull thing
plodding to schools, too circumspect to sing,
too absent-hearted, too absurdly grave.
Not one light smile would limber up my talk.
He left me free to come with wild distaste.
I came to Him. Love called me and I came.
The years since then have stood so shimmering still.
Whole girlhoods of mysterious memories fill
my bones with song, and light a radiant flame
like Van Gogh's Sunny Midi, warm and chaste.

1962.
Published in *Commonweal*, April 19, 1963.

Elegy for Sister Angele

Her funeral went forth in black and white
under December snow. The trees were black
and black and white the nuns went two by two
as white flakes starred her coffin's poor black cloth
and lay like light, cool tears upon my cheeks.
So cold and bright the snow upon the hearse—
Spenser's November Eclogue sang in me:
        "O happy herse!
        Cease now, my muse, now cease thy sorrow's source,
        O joyful verse."

Sing, blessed is the bride the snow falls on
(a carol of death and a verse for her I love).
Snow and star and I echo the poet's song
while formally with knitted shawls and gloves
and Sunday veils worn ceremoniously,
six of us, honored, walked ahead of her
like bridesmaids, though they called us pallbearers.
        "Yet once more, O ye laurels," Milton sang.
        I sang with him and saw the daystar mount.

We walked in snow to where she last would lie
in her white temporal bed—that garden plot.
My grief was joyous at her graveside then.
I said amen to her eternal rest—
the pine tree's empty nest while in the prayer
and winter wind the priest's white pages turned.
A memory of her classroom taught me here.
        Poor Tennyson, bereft, I sing with you:
        "Let death's deep knowledge grow from more to more."

That fleeting smile upon her lifeless mouth
had seemed the passing print her spirit made,
as travelers leave their light prints in the snow
so we may follow them. O gracious hint
like smiles at doorways when a lover comes
and beckons to his love to understand
what blissful greeting waits in the next room.
      As virtuous men pass mildly—she had gone—
      I thought of Donne's first stanza and said : So—
And quoted to the snow against the sky:
      "When I saw what a strict grave could do,
      I saw not why verse might not do so too.
      Verse hath a middle nature; heaven keepes soules,
      The grave keeps bodies, verse the fame enroules.

1962.

Elegy for an Ornithologist

Binoculars unfocus the blurred nests
predicting unrest that precedes migration;
the stir of wing and breast. I think of Bede's
lone swallow whirring through the castle hall
to illustrate life's little length of days.

The ornithologist has turned her gaze.
Lullula arborea, the wood lark,
continues from far groves his nuptial song.
A complex syrinx gives him resonance
with seven pairs of muscles. So she said.

And now the ornithologist is dead.
O birds of Pliny, and of Aristotle,
O Minnesota Loon, O killdeer crying,
spizella passerina in the sun,
(small chipping sparrow), olive vireo.

From a dark tree with two crossed boughs the slow
and sacred disillusionment of death
flashed radically through her eyes, and now
irrevocably caught what gaze of truth
refocuses her love. No hummingbird
in morning-glory so sustains his life.

1960s.
Published in *Sisters Today*, August 1963, p. 1971
and in *Body of Time*, 1971.

Time Is a Bone in the Sun

A place in time is made
by the white shank-bone of the horse
lying low by the stone in the pasture grass
a beautiful emblem now
of the soul of an animal's speed
in the shape of its lines and curves
restraining the motion of change.
The horse of my girlhood's time
forever rides on this wind
in motionless miles of the mind
in the stillness of pastures past
grown clear as the white shank-bone
forever leaping the stone.

A place in time is made
in the clearing that gathers light
from the thin white stump of the chestnut tree,
the bone of the beautiful bole,
the shadowless, open grief
in the grass on the classic slope
where the absent blossoms sway
in the sun of the healing day
a white scar shines in the air
where the dancing branches were.
It is stripped to its soul in the grass.
Stilled in time it becomes
an emotion inward grown
as sharp as the white shank-bone,
the motionless change in the horse,
the change in the tree's still force.

1962.
Published in *Commonweal*, January 12, 1968, p. 186
and in *Body of Time*, 1971.

Reverie at the Site of a Prairie Church

*(for the dedication of Saint Jude's Church
in Thompson, North Dakota)*

I think of Chartres and Cologne,
a cosmopolitan shepherd, and Solomon.
Beyond grow wheatfields.
No one quarries stone.

This is midwest America. Square
and frame, the architecture
of grain elevators evokes
endless wheatfields where

immeasurable horizons outline tall
telephone poles on planes of green.
Men in overalls, bronze in the sun,
build a brick wall.

There will be a spire
as vertical as Notre Dame's
breaking the west winds
just as high and higher

than meadowlarks spiral song.
This temple grows
in weather-skeptical eyes
into a new Jerusalem, a strong-

hold of faith, Eucharist. Blues
of sky and glass supply contemplation's
color. An altar keeps in time a timeless
covenant of love.

1963.

In Memory of Flannery O'Connor

Writing to his immortal son, John Yeats
spoke of the way we all remember death
when we experience deep affection.
This feeling for mortality still grates
upon my Irish heart. The way she said:
"The violent bear it away . . . the lame shall be
first in the kingdom . . ." Prophets, blind, have sung
with friends and kinsmen: "May the angels lead
her into paradise." The day I heard
her death announced, an iridescent image blurred
like peacocks' tails; a radiance of eyes
in my mind's eye. I saw her rise and face
her life's true ambience in an embrace
revealing light. In Christ her story spread.
She who was reticent where angels tread
knew how the peacocks that she farmed could weave
cerulean symbols. All those radiant eyes
rising together in divine surprise!

She'd see it. Then point out a silly head
and publish stories of their raucous cries
knowing this side of heaven symbols leave
a limited perception. Now her eyes perceive
clearly in highlights what we dimly see.

1964.

Appearances: An Elegy for J.L.M.

Where the old homestead's wide, white-pillared porch
runs clear around the house to stop abruptly
as we would, too, before the flower beds,
he watched the summer turning into fall
with all the subtle changes that it made.

The August just before his autumn death
my uncle chose that view for meditation;
laboring to keep up appearances
he was aware and dignified and dear,
saying he was "just fine" when someone asked.

His garden, too, had rallied for its death,
showing its brightest blooms those chilling days,
stubborn as he to hold out signs of life
by way of dahlia and chrysanthemum,
orange and crimson bloom and marigold.
Even the bluest of the morning-glories
climbed the cold wires of his garden fence.

One changing afternoon on the south porch
I watched the sky with him and watched dark clouds
gather and lower over turning trees
and watched the porch swing in its ebb and flow

bearing a four-year nephew up and down
over the floor that slanted like a ship's.

Rain caught the sun that glistened on the leaves
now tough and grey with the long summer's dust.
It freshened us. My uncle's face revealed
the classic shape of final clarity

losing its fleshy outlines, the old flaws,
life's accidents, the wear of everyday
so that the sculptured lines of his long love
came clear and deep like meaning from a poem.
His eyes were on the garden. Then he stood
as one who senses that a ceremony
demands a straighter stance. And when I saw
what he was gazing at I stood up, too.

There was a vivid rainbow in the yard.
It arched the crab trees and the willow grove.
One end of it dipped vaguely through the woods,
the other brushed the bronze chrysanthemums
precisely in the center of the plot.

1964.

Hudson Pilgrimage

Light was given that day
as grace is given without stint,
like a vocation. The everyday morning
shimmers to infinity down all the summer Hudson.

The New York Central tracks the Hudson closely,
taking us on a pilgrimage
through a divine milieu:
beauty and squalor
build and diminish
past Hastings and Yonkers,
warehouses, meadows,
factories and pastures,
present, outdistanced,
until Poughkeepsie stops the New York Central.

When I stood then in St. Andrew cemetery
noon light took Teilhard's new white gravestone
and proclaimed its message among the shimmering leaves
that seemed like green extensions of the river
ascended now to ripple in the sky.

"Petrus Teilhard de Chardin" the cut stone spelled
as if it spoke the world's diaphany
in an absolute white glow, complete
among rows and rows of other green-as-hope graves
and older stones.

Then an acorn fell like a promise
on that last bright August day in 1965.
Ten years had flowed by since his
April burial among these close-budded,
bare spring trees in the Hudson valley.

I gathered up the acorn in an envelope
with grasses cut down in their finite bloom
by novices who spoke in Lebanese.

As I knelt I recalled from the Scriptures
that the field grasses must wither
though there is now and will be always
life from the grave.

1965.

Plato: A Girl's Thought

Caught in the dialectic of a doubt
the heart beats yes and no the way a girl
will pull the daisy petals for reply:
"He does. He does not love. He does. Does not."

And when the "yes" is plucked, the sun comes out.
The daisy center, golden with its seed
is all that's left. The future is a flower,
the doubt resolved in one round golden aye.

1965.
Published in *Commonweal*, March 5, 1965, p. 733.

What You Hear

1.

This utterance, hesitant,
flutters between thoughts, skirting
ineffable lights, yet hoping to be
as open as windows revealing the darkness.

This reticence circles a heart's
inviolate memories
as a bird will circle its sacred place
against trespassers; its song
a barbed wire fence in the air, its throat
wild with dismay for the threatened treasure.

Delicately, in time, thought and utterance may
shift into place, into words forming
the heart's subliminal message,
its intimate truth, its love and its wound.

2.

What you hear is the heart's sound
disoriented, seeking
its meaning, sequence, consequence.

What phrase, after all, can express the effect
riven, in time, from the very heart of its cause?
What word can ever express this
ineffable grief, its light and its wisdom?

1965.

The Mind Is Its Own Shape

Sometimes it is like a shell
convoluted, and heard
only when the enchanted ear held
it close enough to catch the sea-tones
deep with silences.

Or alone in its cage of bone the mind
sings like Saint Mechtild's nightingales and larks.

Or shapes a circle like a golden ring
with facets of sapphire blue in the crystal planes
of stones.

A mind can be as tall as a spire
catching the weather to inquire the winds.

Again the mind is moulded to freedom
open as bells
curved wide through mid-air
where all weathers tone it
and time varies the tones
rings it true to the tongues telling.

Often a mind is like a flower
calyx closing and opening
in all colors
taking the sun in
reflecting the light
quietly
and the rain.

Or it is shaped like a whole meadow of essences
holding the odor of sweet grasses
and the graces of summer
as well as the cold clarity of the snow
with its fruit-blue, eloquent shadows.

Your mind is a mystery to me
like a sky full of birds singing and soaring
and clouds moving colors of pearls and seas
with the sun always there in the center golden
and the moon gentle among the faithful stars.
Tops of trees pattern it
austere or flowering,
sheltering.

Your mind is humble and high
like the everyday and unearthly sky
in the shape of light.
It is like the deep blue night that I trust
when I close my eyes.

Like faith, like the shape of prayer.

Reprinted from *America*, January 30, 1965,
with permission of America Press, Inc. c 1965.
All rights reserved.
Published in *Body of Time*, 1971.

Three Acts of Love

"To write the poem is an act of love."
—Dorothy Sayers, *The Mind of the Maker*

1.   In the Meadow

We kept our distance, delicately near
as lovers in familiar reverence,
with eyes made holy, open as the hand
that lifts a sacred gift in sacrifice.

Such was the gesture of our bones and flesh
before the black-eyed-susan and the moth--
lest from the weight of our admiring gaze
we should unbalance with a heavy glance
the lovely dance of butterfly and weed,
the still mobility of autumn love
poised in the self-possession of all giving.

2.   In the Garden

Changing and changeless under mobile skies
in the recurring gardens of September
love still creates what we in hope remember:
chrysanthemums are brought to their perfection,
our shadows move toward noon in one direction,

the rose to earth, the earth to rose is given,
the seeds of time grow our continuous heaven
changeless and changing under mobile skies.

3.   Before the Sunflower

Our earth explains our God. Daphne's myth
told ancient Greeks something about Apollo
who made immobile movements of her flight
as proof that gods make fruitful yes or no.
She, his swift love, became the green-boughed laurel.

The myth explaining us explains our God.
Within the daily round like the sunflower
we grow erect and taller than we are
corrected by His light the livelong day,
our motivation in His golden Face.

1965.
Published in *Commonweal*, November 26, 1965, p. 236.

Flourishes: For a Friend Absent in Autumn

"There is a world of difference between
forgetting and remembering."

From V. Woolf's *A Writer's Journal.*

Summer's Time winds down; gardens run
counterclockwise into memory. Along the walks
rows of bright trumpets play to the soul's ear,
The mind's eye. Purple flutes of petunias
blow their soft flourishes. Green leaves
crisp into metal. The whitest green quivers
in winds. Pink petunias flare
clear as the clarion red, the striped, the white.

My thought runs counterclockwise
into memory where time abides. I am led
by this last vivid flourish of trumpets,
fluted petunias, to your far doorstep. I find you
at home in your doorway whistling Haydn's
Trumpet Concerto or Mozart's piece
for flute and strings. These notes, the petunia's flourish,
open the way to you. A clear glance
of sentience and affection brings
to brief perfection my time-fractured world.

1965.

Light Parable I: For Robert

The blue glass pitcher fills with light
on the window sill
spills a shimmer of sky on the wall
creating a new light, textured from glass,
formed by the shape of the mouth,
the rim and the color of it.

Light pours through it wholly.
Morning flows inside and out.

This is the parable of amorphous light:
filling the inner and outer shape of your life
it overflows;
spills your own version of day
on all the walls of your world.

1966.
Reprinted from *America*, April 22, 1967, with
permission of America Press, Inc. c 1967.
All rights reserved.
Published in *Body of Time*, 1971.

Pomegranate Seeds on Christmas Morning

*The narcissus flower . . . signifies divine beauty which here below appears in
the form of the beauty of the world, as a snare for the soul. Then he gives
a pomegranate seed to eat—whereby the soul is captured forever. The
pomegranate seed is the consent which the soul gives to God almost without
knowing it and without admitting it to itself. This is an infinitely small
thing and yet it decides its destiny forever.*
—Simone Weil, *Intimations of Christianity*

Having seen lately the noble gold sunflower

become a disc of brown seed, a shallow bowl

where the chickadees feed their song,

having walked lately a meadow among

brittle weed pods, innumerable

imaginative shapes of death

that every year become delicate promises,

and knowing that under the snow now

the meadow is pure with want,

that in this season the hidden god

is the life of all flowering,

as the Greeks knew it I know.

And I have come this winter morning to the table

ripe for the gift of a pomegranate.

Its gold-pink sections carry seeds

as rose-red as its rind.

The myth springs from old roots,

a destiny, a Word

sown darkly in my mind.

I recall Demeter as I eat.

A sense of her mourning and joy

turns this ordinary table into Eleusinian fields

where I, Persephone, am sought forever by the god

whose snare is beauty, the narcissus flower

whose beauty is an irresistible power

wholly impelling me to catch at it roots and all,

its petals divinely blue

and smelling of every spring

and future freshness that keeps recurring

through underworlds of winter-seeking-spring

in life-long life-longing.

Reprinted from *America*, December 23-30, 1967,
with permission of America Press, Inc. c 1967.
Published in *Body of Time*, 1971.

To Stop the Rose

Without the world within, no world without
can keep that first June rose within your hand
permanent amid impermanence.

The swift diminishing of summer days,
the fall of petals on the table top
begins to say what the stripped winter says
about the withering of this world's ways.

Without the world within, no eye could stop
the rose's doom or keep pure bloom in thought
as I keep that June morning's perfect rose
to stop the rose from falling from its prime.

In worlds without, all flowers come to naught
nor could our long green-growing memory mime
this world of roses for our winter time
without the world within your eyes and mine.

By roadside fields green-growing parallels
sliding together in the distance prove
the paradox of parallels that touch.

For parallels do touch in our far gaze.
Fact and illusion are both ways to truth.
The distant touching of our separate ways
is mine from worlds within from other days.

Without the world within, the small green worm
that spun his summer journey from the tree
could not secure his web so subtly free
within my consciousness that I could see
him wind new webs upon a summer wind
to bind that June day to eternity
Where worlds without are saved by worlds within
with leaf and rose and field anemone
and all things in their prime—and you and me.

1967.

Sabbatical in New York City

1. Light fell in rain as the leaves fell
bright leaves gave up their stores of sun
for me to plant my pilgrim feet upon.
Reversing photosynthesis
the leaves shone back their living light through death.

During migration a monarch butterfly
drowned in the ocean off Coney Island.
And in the Bronx another monarch fell
in faultless symmetry to the cement.
The fluid death and dry descent occurred
miles from where prize dahlias stirred
and fell to seed in the garden.

Snow fell in a dance of wind
shining the sky out of countenance.
Walking on structured crystal I meditated:
must fallen transparencies
become opaque, hard, pedestrian?

2. Though crocus bulbs in subway stations
sprout from their round glazed pots
these green prophets stop only one out of
a hundred hurrying men.
Their price forbids this kind of grand impatience.
Real springtime costs the patience of the poor.

I dream:
dragonfly over lilypond
like shimmering aircraft, noiseless
blue-streaked submarine;
stillness in motion
reflecting
peace with opening flowers between.

Is heaven-on-earth revealed thus in the City?
Separately, together
two worlds turn in my mind.
I live in both as pilgrim-resident.

1960s.

Bronx Neighborhood

Petunias swim the ground
floating pink on green
between cement and stone.

Sunflower, myrtle, rose
not one rare inch of soil
without its hum of bees.

In dooryards three feet wide
each side a tangled walk
rise cosmos, hollyhocks,

fence-framed in iron scrolls
steep steps as old as stone
(a tenement Bonnard).

In one yard that I pass
I see a cripple doze
head down, in twisted bones

breathing a flower-sky
as labored as the green
that struggles against streets

harsh with the day's debris
and near as death to him—
glass broken, empty tins

where I, a pilgrim, walk
to keep my heart alive
among the flowering homes.

1968.
Published in *Commonweal*, November 15, 1968, p. 256.

Time Keeps What Is Its Own

Let us in time be everything we are.
Our flexible fine limbs that dance and love,
our shouting, whispering, wisdom-kissing lips,
our eyes receiving beauty, playing back,
shall with old ferns and fish and fallen trees
dissolve in time's deep veins of radiant stone.
Time, from the outside, keeps what is its own.

Let us in time give everything because
time keeps not you nor me who from our birth
keep time inside us as biography.
Let us move forward on bright cycling suns
aware that as we keep time with our pulse
we are by time unwound, on shadowed ground
drying to wrinkles like a summer's fruit
dissolving in the earth to build the stone.
Time has no time for what is not its own.

Within our perishable veins the skeins
of steadfast love and thoughts like poetry
forever fail to focus in our bones'
hard, narrow structures. Open mystery we
whose other, inner time, biography
transcend time's stone, resist time's gravity.
Though we keep time, time keeps not you nor me.
Time has no time for what is not its own.

1968.

51

What Do We Learn By Heart?

Is there an answer that we cannot hear
when the engine is running? When this smooth
maroon motor, assembled in womb-darkness for the embarking
pumps steadily in our breasts
are we more truly at sea than we know?

Soon we feel the pride of pumping through choppy seas,
steering straight on; the exhilarating speed,
high waves whipping our sides; and after a calm
the pride of pulsing through blinding, noon-bright waters
to satisfy that voyage paradigm guiding the pilgrim mind
so that we sail at joy's subtle bidding on and on and on.
Does not this effort of the heart imply forever?

And while this mortal muscle, heart, propels us
it keeps time in place, transforms earth-fuel into sailing grace;
its red-blue circuit empowers lips, tongues, eyes,
ears, hands, and thighs: all that we love by we steer by
when joy on the horizon shimmers against immortal skies.
Sighting it we are geared for this passage.

When we cry out then is not "heart" the core metaphor
of all our language? It connotes life-surge, suggests fruit:
apple, pear, grape; our food is earth-truth:
sun-centered continuity, present rooted in past,
stemming toward future. So heart, the valved engine
engenders language which is our power; cries, takes breath, is born,
loves, prays; and speech flowers, bequests, breathes death
they say. But this is my question:

If this pilgrim man, earth-angel, heart-engined mind
stops soaring and sailing and singing and crying
when the generating muscle runs down, shuts off—
what of all that light, all this delight
let into the mind through the veined eyes, tongues, lips,
ears, hands, and thighs? What of thought—what of love
experienced in time as timeless? When the engine stops
shall we hear then the transcendent answer?

1968.

Audubon's Hummingbird:
note for a history of gratitude

It came to pass in Kentucky
on blue-grass ground
that a bird-catching spider
drew its web strand by strand
around a nectar-feeding hummingbird

close by the crepe myrtle
a bird-watcher
severed the deadly web with a deft hand
and freed the brilliant nectar-feeding bird

which then in mid-flight turned
with just an exquisite instinct to guide her
and brushed with recognition that kind
hand.

James John Audubon, the naturalist
recorded this that evening in his journal.
rooted in pots of earth.

1960s.
Published in *Commonweal*, August 19, 1969, p. 191
and in *Body of Time*, 1971.

Nun with Young Girls in an Art Gallery

"All things are kept in being by their yearning
for their own beauty."

—Pseudo-Dionysius

Yearning for their own beauty
they slide past the Virgin
and Saints in their glory
to stop poised and stern
before the white nudes
of Modigliani.

Yearning dilates their eyes
darkly as they appraise
woodland moods of Corot.

Before Jan Vermeer's
Woman Reading a Letter
yearning parts their young lips
distance slips through their eyes
spirit-still like a long
shadow in sun.

I watch who have gazed
yearning sternly as they
at the virgin and saints
in this high labyrinthine
mirror of life
with its multiple doorways.

1969.
Published in *Commonweal*, January 10, 1969, p. 469
and in *Body of Time*, 1971).

Part 3
Poems of the 1970s

"A way of seeing shapes a way of being"
— from *Preference*, 1975

The Stems of Flowers Are the Pillars of the World

Tempered by weather
welded by sun rays and metallic rain
the stems of flowers rise, poised,
erect as pillars they hold the world up.

Light-power, stronger than stone or steel
channels through leaf-scrolls
along each live green column
direct to its capital flower
joining the sky.

Each inevitable design
is a tenuous reminder
of the pillar of inner worlds: fidelity.
How it grows erect from a heart's rectitude,
the seed selecting elements for growing
true to its form
draws cell by cell to its quality,
color, texture,
reaches its height.

Indispensable for the holding up of the world
as stems of flowers, the heart's fidelity.
The delicate stems of bluebells, true to themselves
are pillars of the universe, as you are,
as the rose and the gladiola,
lilac-bole, apple tree, oak and sequoia,
their protein strength gently holding
the world to its height, to its life-sheltering.

1970.
Published in *Body of Time*, 1971.

Passage à la Poe

. . . How each visitor shall confess the sad valley's restlessness . . .
(Edgar Allan Poe, *The Valley of Unrest*)

Elusive day forever yields its light
shadow by lengthening shadow into night
as petals blacken on the velvet rose
and the white, fleeting feet of beauty pass
over the mortal grass without repose.

What always is lies elsewhere. Beauty's rhyme
sets echoes ringing beyond space and time.
The pilgrim's journey is his beating heart
marking the tempo of his pulse and song
in formal measures. Time and space become
a future entered and a going from,
a throbbing movement, restless pendulum
swung between grief and gladness all life long.
In his recurrent sorrow he must keep
mourning the beauty he would wake from sleep,

from death-like sleep, a silence deep and dark,
earth-bound as seeds bind flowers when the spark
of vivid darting movement pales in death.
Mourning, the poet makes of grief a song
and wakes his love with music, beauty's breath.

1971.
In program for the opera, *The Voyage of Edgar Allan Poe* by
Dominick Argento, performance April 24, 1976 (published
by North Central Publishing Co. 1971).

Beauty—A Character Sketch

Beauty is well-bred and asks nothing
but that the other be delighted and at ease,
freely left to wonder before a living ocean,
flights of river-spanning ridges, groves of nourishing orange trees.

She welcomes casually, from doorsteps smiling
with everyday homeland love that a child can endure.
Those facts of her nature unfathomable, rich, disturbing,
she keeps for lovers, suffering, subtle and mature.

With views as vast as seas and firmament
she greets with peace the hurried, crowded gaze
of those who seek her in perplexities.
With the sky's energies she lights the days

with high intent, creating deep content
and discontent. Things ordered and divined
are secrets open as a tree or flower;
a recognition in the poet's mind

of courtesies expected, true, surprising.
In song and conversation she is heard:
meadowlark, Pergolesi, friends: her phrasing
freely endears the listener to her word.

Published in *Commonweal*, January 15, 1971, p. 370.

Where the Sun Lifts

Snow ascends invisibly. Mild air
releases from hard white stars moist
shimmering atmosphere. The sun warmly
draws its bright breath. Ascensions everywhere

begin with death. Have begun where the sun lifts
white patch by patch from black woods into clouds.
(Envision saints soaring to heaven like doves.)
Up the slopes the sharp-lobed hepatica drifts

and up through the brown matted grasses the white
snow-trillium shifts old, sodden leaves.
"Man lives himself into the boundless;" his earth
is dust struck with sun into flowering light.

Published in *Body of Time*, 1971.

The First Thaw

Snow ascends invisibly. Mild air
releases from hard white stars moist
shimmering atmosphere. The sun warmly
drawing its bright breath. Ascension everywhere

begin with death; have begun where the sun lifts
white patch by patch from black woods into clouds
(envision saints into heaven like doves). On the slope
sharp-lobed hepatica stirs. And snow-trillium shifts

fallen wet oak leaves; lifts living white
petals through crusts of old snow. ("A man lives
his way into the boundless"). Remember that earth
is dust struck with light into flower. And hope.

Published in *Commonweal*, January 15, 1971, p. 370.

A Poem of Cold Fires

for William of Ghana

1.

How, in the Fanti tongue
are the fireflies named?
When I described them in my letter
you replied
as formally as in a poem
that word of their vague nebulae
beyond my windowed wall in Illinois
kindled this memory:
Nets spread among night-green vines
in the grasslands of Ghana
where you, a child,
caught their cold fire in your hands
to uncover their light's source.

What name did you call them?

2.

Those constellations of the woods,
the wild asters
burn the last warm violet from my world
and kindle here with gentle grace
the loneliness of this no-place.
On brittle stems they light the autumn brush
with mild, thin rays
flickering one by one
into a brown oblivion.

I break from the nearest stalk the brightest flower.
Its light will last until my walk is over.

Published in *Commonweal*, April 2, 1971, p. 87
and in *Body of Time*, 1971.

If Space Is the Body of Time

Before light broke into mauve and red
gainst the mountain peaks at morning
you woke, you said, to luminescence.

A shimmering whiteness throbbed
against the dark
uniting night with day
in reminiscence of
the body's behaviour in love.

If space is the body of time
music becomes the mode through which we sense
the beating of its heart as of our own.
Mozart and Beethoven
composed in time the personal transience
of those perfections that we come upon
surprised and hovering, other than ourselves:
beauty's recurring transience, and light's
throbbing in unity with what we are.

Published in *Body of Time*, 1971.

Reflection on a Library Window-Sill

In the reference room
a window-sill's granite slabs
absorb, reflect
as if within the slow
and grey-brown surface of a stream
the temporal slopes of snow
among the trees beyond the wide window.

They are caught there, whiter than clouds
and shadowed blue,
holding the black trees' branches
upright and flaring. A surreal dream
in polished stone
they seem to hear the vague
flecked shapes of fossil leaves
adrift without falling.

Among lavender auras clouds stream:
a procession in process. Time
is earth revealed
as in this granite window-sill reflecting
aeons within the polished stone;
reflecting change impervious to my touch
absorbing all the movements of the woods,
the slow, unceasing process of the sky.

Published in *Body of Time*, 1971.

A Poem of Windless Snow

Three windless days and nights of falling flakes
cast snow bells over the mountain-ash berries;
lily-cups over the red-orange clusters.

This is poetry that a fathomless sky makes
for the eye alone. Earthly vocabularies
are not fine and light enough to ring so lustrous

a tone. As in a child's dream
the imperfect world lies healed of its imperfection.
Its leafless trees bear boughs of crystal light;

its luminous green flows white where the evergreen
cascades serenely in the bright direction
of slopes and paths that illumine even the night.

in this shimmer of unity a world of wounds
transfigures silently under bells that glow.
Children fall without hurt in a dream of snow.

Published in *Body of Time*, 1971.

Seventy-Two Ways of Receiving Light

Anyone very much alive might see
that there are seventy-two shades of green
on the one tree.

Alive to the finger tips anyone might
distinguish leaf from leaf's light-
sensitivity;
touch each leaf separately and feel
which qualities absorbed to what degree
the rays of the sun
to make these greens deep, rich, pale, bright
in seventy-two ways of receiving light.

A-light with life anyone might perceive
rising in autumn's leaves
the ghosts of all these shades of green
at last transmuted to the bright
clear color of light
burning in shapes of flame
at one with all light again.

Published in *Body of Time*, 1971.

Perfection: A Litany at My Mother's Grave

A lifetime is paid, sight unseen, for that
simple necessity we call perfection.

Belief, hope, love are trifocal lenses
the human spirit wears to examine
this fact and that: new-born hands,
a first anemone, a snowflake on the coat,
dew on millet, flax blue, ripe wheat,
the movement of well-bred cats among
bric-a-brac, the grace of a Nureyev,
the compassionate face of a Mother Teresa,
the light-field Hyades in late May—

We make long litanies of hopes, goads and guesses.
I add Mozart's Concerti, a dog's nose, an elegant
mountain,
sounds and glimpses, statements of sheer belief
received continuously in love by the alert heart
building its expectations. Nothing will do
but to pay one's life out for perfection,
breath by breath.

1973.

69

Elegy for Colleen for Whom Time Was Music

Life alters
death by death.
October burns
into November;
all its bright-veined life drains
from rose and dahlia, petal, leaf, and stem;
withdraws from grasses, from the apple tree.

Beauty and fruit plucked here in time by time.

Late summer's sun moved
further day by day
from your piano in the living room
leaving your music in shadow.
Piles of time-worn scores
with all their time—kept grace therein
held in such rich abeyance: Scarlatti, Bach,
Ravel, Chopin
composing constantly the sound of life's
sorrow and joy, its light and darkness. Love, its
suffering and death.

You'd phrased them once to sound's perpetual
perishing eternal as you played. And then

Under October sun your time had come.

The gold of elm trees flamed,
bronze scrolls of oak leaves shone
as your soul's finest metal, forged in pain,
shone on your last all time-consuming day
timeless and true as any masterpiece.

1974.

Snowdrift

When my father swept me
in one almighty sweep
from the blue cold of the snowdrift
to his woolen shoulder, my numb cheeks
comforted against his beaver cap,
my snow-caked leggings limbered,
chapped knuckles kissed, he imbued
thenceforward to this day the drifts
of every winter snow
with feelings soft as fur
and warmed them with the smoulder of his pipe
(his love) a sense of home.
The heart's vocabulary builds
like this: a list of meanings rubbed
from love at hand as personal as touch.

1975.
Published in *Commonweal*, July 21, 1978, p. 455.

Preference

". . . the seeing depends ever on the being . . ."
Thoreau in his *Writer's Journal*

The ivy binds the light into green arrows
and trails itself in time from its dark roots
arrow by arrow into greener life.

A way of seeing shapes a way of being.

Each preference stirs a pulsing dynamo
of heart-beat, light-wave, turning each impulse
wholly toward what it is, the being, true,

communing through mysterious preferences,

unswerving as a bee hailed by its flowers,
seeming erratic, choosing and forgetting,
retracing its cross-pollinating flight,

the field of choice a providence of light.

1975.
Published in *Commonweal*, June 20, 1975, p. 205.

Lines from a Primitive

Though I could not read words
I could read oak trees. I could
know from these the meaning of
roots and stability.

I could read the movement of squirrels
and birds; though I could not read words
I could infer from wings and limbs
the time-hinged meaning of mobility.

I could read the light-drawn rising of
the vine and rose; the shades of meaning each stem
shows; and I could study what the small seeds
mean
and learn directly all that grows from them.

Yet if I could not read
the knowledge words impart
how could I shake my belief
that the elm's death and the earth's quake
reveal the same life-shattering grief
the body feels at insults to the heart?

1976.

Published in *Commonweal*, March 4, 1977, p. 135.

Watching the Olympics

They show us in slow motion how
in the perfect action each movement
is ever righting itself in respect
to the other, in respect to the earth
and the space and their laws
from balance to point of balance
the enduring bones leap,
the muscles remember
the rules of flexible elegance,
integrity, grace.

With hearts as with bodies
it is grace that wins every contest;
that survives judgment
day in and day out
as when two persons (or nations)
long pledged to each other
in marriage or friendship
learn to move freely together
forever achieving their balance;
fluid, enduring.

1976.
Published in *Commonweal*, August 5, 1977, p. 404.

On Falling Silent

*We cannot ever know whether this or that which grieves us is not
the secret principle of our later joy.*
—Leon Bloy

Nothing hurts so much as this brief glimpse
of a heart's beauty.
A sudden kindness, temperate and true
leaves wounds as sharp and clean
as love's rare answer coming from afar
piercing the stern wall between earth and heaven.
The tears that rise
resemble dew upon the warm chilled bloom
the way it forms from contrasts in the air.

There is no other way to voice
the grief that brings this calm
than to fall silent, gazing at the wall.

1978.

The Marvelous

The reason why the philosopher may be likened to the poet is this: they are both concerned with the marvelous. Thomas Aquinas

1.

They're not in thrall to things, but weave in freedom
the strands of their thoughts . . . like webs . . .
open . . . delicate . . . disciplined nets of connections
spinning from inner threads
catching and holding between leaves
between flowers . . . between
steps of a staircase . . . corners of ceilings . . .
between frames of their windows and doors . . .

Their webs of thought compose limits, filter lights,
catch dewdrops that round and fill and break
into colors. They discover coincidences
that occur again and again and are marvelous as when
the sun strikes dust in the rain in the sky
at an angle creating in reference to earth
the colors, the curve of the rainbow.

2.

Indoors the geometry of a blackboard
draws their gaze to the ends of the garden where they see
the rectangle living its discipline,
constant and possible, where
nothing's allowed to compete with the life of the flower.

Ratios compose their thoughts. Angle by angle
they measure a truth to equal its meaning,
finding the language.

In a kitchen they contemplate
the unerring silver curve of a pitcher. How it mirrors
squares of bright sky curtained at windows
and a room scaled to surprise the eye.
Their minds take pleasure in
a little leather pouch that's full of stones.
Their semi-precious smoothness in the hand
suggests wonders, transformations,
reality touched at the core. As when
gladiolas from the market, fresh
white and red form an analogy
for beauty's brevity. For them
all nature matches thoughts that strike the heart.

Their minds rest in the marvelous, refreshed:
a harmony of flowered cups . . . hands pouring coffee
passing croissants and preserved cherries:
courtesy's elegant formulae equating gestures, artifacts, words,
the a,b,c's that will prove equal to
the moving, constant x,y,z's of love.

1978.

Elm Tree and Other Shadows

The elm at the corner is down;
   chips of its tall life fragments in the snow
      scattered at random from those rings of years.

The substance of the shadow's branch is gone
   that gave my wall its morning play of grace
      the year around and made leaf, branch and bird

a presence in my room. Now this profound
   removal changes everything in sight.
      The window frames become

straight shadows of themselves
   in sun. Through empty panes of light
      my random memories gather shade on shade

the substance of the elm to set it down.

1978.

When Time Is Ripe

Down the familiar road each rut
is a revelation
full of its secrets.

As when time is ripe each day
there is something to be understood
which cannot be understood
completely.

A leaf lifts from its branch
and falls red and gold
at a message of weather
a wind with an edge.
And that is never the end. Repeatedly
new things happen. Time ripens
again and again. The fruit fills
and numbers of birds gather,
flights mapped in their systems, their wings
imprinted with certainties
telling them summer will follow.

It is all predictable
and surprising, the weather's direction
the rut and the wrinkling pod
the sun-mapped wings of the robin.

1978.

Bonheur

Like an amateur botanist I love to examine the roots of things, admire
the tethered way they float green life far and wide between
earth and sky. Each root is original-shallow or deep in its reach.
The diffuse roots of mature rye run three hundred miles (and then some)
creating a webbed network throughout the fields, like alfalfa. In coulees
the cattail, in marshes the lily, the marigold. In ditches the wild rose,
thistle, anemone. There's the Bushveld's acacia, California's redwood,
the desert's yucca, cacti. The oak of the temperate zone. Such wonders!
I feel their roots tapping the stream of the poet in me; their
xylem and phlegm magnified in my eyes until nothing but praises
flow from the microscope into my pencil's poem.

Later, I see

that a root's flower breaks apart in its modest or brilliant
heart. Becomes a continual *alpha* and *omega*. Soon I'll draw
a poet's conclusions—which is to say
I'll leave the question of roots as open as tulips, as
lilies or columbine, bleeding heart, bluebells and all
that's rooted to rise and change, to grow and to
flower and waken high hopes in the heart.

These high hopes! They tease me
to shift to the question of happiness, search out its roots
which seem fragile as moods. Happiness! The word seems wrong
for the feeling I've linked with it. How can its small root, "hap" (chance)
amass the flowering I mean when I wish you happiness?
Is there a word for it? Felicity (its root, "felix") is too intense for

the everyday tiding over from pain, absence, weariness, lack of élan. "Felix"
sends up a certain bloom of bliss. But I, for one,
couldn't live with it in this world. And fortune's roots
(fors and ferre) corrupt in Lake Tahoe, break apart
on the wheels of Las Vegas. Where, then, is the "hap," the chance
of happiness? The fortune? The felicity? What strong and fruitful root
can name what I wish for you? I don't know. I prefer
to wish you "Bonheur"—its root from Old French
trailed into Middle English gathering
the good I wish you each hour breaking into its appropriate flower between
heaven and earth where you live.

1978.

At a Friend's House

As with affection the morning sun sheds
a new light on things
without changing them.

Examples: in the light of it
the daylily, folded against the wall
is touched into flame.

From its everyday shade
the midsummer apple tree
shimmers with highlights

And each petunia, common, ubiquitous,
shows itself singular
royal and brilliant, purple and red.

As with the morning sun affection
sheds a new light on the common,
the folded, the everyday spirit;

Rests its attention
in stillness and depth
and reveals what is loved.

1978.

Transplanted

Impatiens that take full summer sun
in open beds well-tended on the lawn
will tolerate low light within a room
at summer's end will glow like lamps in bowls
or grow in winter's north-light on a shelf

as, when the chill of absence strikes the heart
and the full sun of love moves on its course
the vivid growing beauty of its joy
must be transplanted to a distant room
where north-light filters in through memory,

the summer presence cultivated there
its radiance kept patiently in bloom.

1979.

In Praise of Bulbs

Wrapped up in itself the onion's solid bulb is
strong to eye, nostril, and tongue. It stings and
bites; is crisp, white luminous under
paper-thin layers of lavender skin.

Narcissus, wrapped up in itself rests until
light loosens its tight bulb and coaxes its leaves
up from a low bowl of pebbles holding
a flow of water. In due time
informed with its fragrance it blooms
purple, blue, pink, white.

In layers of brown, bud, the crocus bulb
wraps itself against winter. A light sleeper,
it's roused by the sun's far glance at the frozen earth;
bridges the distance left between winter and spring, its
gold/lavender bloom furry and fresh.

A myth-maker, the amaryllis waits
wrapped in its dark bulb, at rest until
time summons it. Then, with spectacular
olympic haste its stems quicken and race
allegro, vivace, presto! It springs tall,
vivid, magnificent, crimson, white: a myth-maker,
all wonder and grace.

1979.

Part 4
Poems of the 1980s

"Our earth explains our God"
— from *Three Acts of Love,* 1986

The Measure: On Coming Home from Abroad

Time is mid-morning in mid June
and place a grey house facing north.
Event: a welcoming embrace.
All else is nothing worth

if this were not, which salvages
the poetry of what I found
that might inform, instruct, amuse
or dazzle and astound:

the Barbican; the Stone of Scone;
the garden of St. Thomas More;
the room where Johnson's lexicon
has come to be; time's lovely lore

in the museum that enshrines
the Elgin Marbles, ransomed gems;
great galleries of Turner skies;
Westminster Bridge; the shimmering Thames.

These take new meaning from my view
of home's small garden; swallows' grace;
the morning-glory's eastern wall;
a spreading screen of pine-green lace.

This trace of Kensington and Kew
my native sky takes measure of
lighting the world within my mind
unbounded and at home with love.
The river is moving gravely after the moon
between the sea and London.

1980.

The Law of Light, the Image Seen, Unseen

1.
Geraniums that fade from their place on the balcony floor.
The light that shaped them recedes,
withdraws red bloom, velour leaves
subtly frilled and two-toned, stalks
rooted in pots of earth.
        Near the glass door
the petunias, true white, pale yellow and red
woven like silken trumpets frail and bright
absorbing light all day through nurturing leaves
are now in turn absorbed by night instead.

This law of light conceals, reveals the moon
and all its vital influence with the sea.
In the dark wood that smoulders on a hearth
the law of light enkindles what has aged
releasing flames that dance and charm a room.

Seen and unseen in time's dark shimmering streams
the law of light, intrinsically obeyed
by all that lives and dies, is imaged here
in sensitive revisions endlessly
extending revelations, shadows, dreams
where we reflect out season's brevity.

The light that ages our attentive eyes,
strains our entranced hearts. Intensely pure
it fades the fine designs we weave ourselves.
The dark becomes light's poor nonentity.
Just visibly bonding death to life
it lifts the anchors that our spirits drop
into the sea of loved reality.

2.
In light of this your presence in the light,
now actually known and loved becomes
a sacred passage into and beyond
my fragile synapse-leaping memory.
The photographs I focus in the sun
cannot in this one moment show your self.
Nor can the videotapes my senses run
at life's electric speed reveal your life's
true image given, centered in the heart
that verifies eternal light in you.

1982.

Chrysanthemums: Between All Saints and All Souls Day

1.
In our northern latitude
old bricks radiate warm tones. Across them
the stripped vine branches trace a script
of finally wrought scrolls for our instruction.

On All Saints Day the south wall
is signed with chrysanthemums, their golden name
formed from a Greek root. In ascending layers
the classic petals taper,
brushing the chill air of November with crisp rays
like icons in winter's anteroom. They shine there
with a rich austerity, their haloes
gracing long stems, brittle for breaking
though they remain flexible, bending and rising
like elegant old bones. Around them
the incense of autumn wreathes subtly
from delicate incised leaves that are pungent,
praiseworthy. *"Gaudeamus omnes
in Domino . . ."*

In my room now sophisticated rich tones
of mature blooms mingle unobtrusively,
tawny and bronze or yellow as winter's light
among shades of wine that approach that
of fine burgundy. *"Munera tibi,
Domine . . ."*

2.
We are between All Saints and All Souls Day.
Your love spreads its light through my meditation,
shifting the shadow of your absence
into an insight as blinding as tears, as astringent
as winter's cold winds, starkly revealing
death's inseparable holy ties
with the deathless joy of the heart,
the radiant peace and the flower, the inspiration.
And yet I pray as the light broods into darkness,
"*De profundis clamavi*
Ad te, Domine . . ."

A faraway lonely clamor
arises high in the northern skies
as an arrowhead soars to the south,
the disciplined flight of wild geese. At their cry
my heart, listening, lifts in its freedom
as in the Gregorian chant of a burial day the unadorned
clear cry of the neumes, ascends through the moving words,
the "*lux aeterna luceat eis, Domine . . .*"
rising and falling to rest
in disciplined rhythm like wings
shaping the tone of my prayer
into pure intuitions of heaven.
"*Justorum animae in manu Dei sunt . . .*"

"*In paradisum . . .*"

1982.

The World at Hand Imagined, Given Back

With cross-stitches the fingers prick
a pattern of angular figures;
with french-knots they wind
stamens of flowers. With infinitesimal
running stitches
kept close as secrecy
the fingers trace the entwining leaves
of an appliqué
while the mind dreams
interpretations of vines.

The style defines itself unconsciously.
The shuttle's voice will tell its hidden schemes.

With quick needles and fine threads the spirit
is weaving its observations, drawing
connections, inconclusive, open,
from text and memory, from color and tone
as it feels the experience: its starkness
black and white, the skeins of gold,
its brush with happiness, the flake of snow,
the water bird migrating, secret death,
the mystery in each answer questioning.

A world translated, distanced, and its themes
weaving through music, novels, poetry,
sculpture and painting or a tapestry

with perfect intervals of bough and bloom

1982.

For the Time Being: The Breath of Life

While light in this loam bed
sweeps Grecian windflowers into color,
gravity moves blue lavender pink white petals
into the summer day's ephemera.

On my knees I sort weed from flower.
My eyes and hands discriminate as I work,
noting the homely messages of time,
so small, so commonplace, so luminous:
a book of hours comforting to read.

On a clear day when the blue
lavender of the ageratum glows along bordered walks, I see why,
though its Greek name translated "ageless," the ageratum
is known commonly as "mist" or "floss." It forms low clouds
of serene lavender drifting with blue over the green
where light reaches to the heart of life "for the time being."

That's a phrase we use lightly. "For the time being,"
we say. Its meaning too profound to probe
while the heart is at work enfolding its own mystery,
unfolding its own perfect accomplishment: "life" as it shapes "love,"
"love" as it fills "life" and becomes
"the breath of life," the words containing more than they can tell.

"The breath of life" we call the elan that animates our best days.
The loss of it changes our breath to sighs
as when the light falls too heavily on our heads
and becomes a burden. Or when a petal's fullness

weighs upon its own delicate beauty and it falls
from its flower.
Everything I love is at risk. I call upon
the intensive care of heaven and hospital to repair
your heart's beat, systole, diastole
in rhythm with your life-task, keeping pace.

"Never mind" you'd say. (Another of those phrases
expressing human wisdom, patience.) Perhaps you'd add,
"Time's fragments will be knit up finally."

My heart in response
sighs to its inseparable spirit, "Be still and know"
and breathes its prayer, its fear of loss, its praise:
"Save this for me," it cries, "Save this.
So loved, so frail. Oh, let it be. Let be
the only one like this in all the world."

My longing like an angel comforts me.
Time being what it is it promises . . .

1983.

Inside-out and Outside-in

Where last week
truck wheels turned and tore the lawn
those night-black scars have healed.

Earth suffers and will suffer long
its two elms, felled.
Air suffers the diminishing red blur,
the cardinal's flight; that loss,
and his bright song.

It will not be too long
when out there
beyond the footlights of first snow
our spirits will applaud the winter's white
uncomfortable gift, its unadorned
austerity, its stark black trees,
its mystery inside-out and outside-in,
its brilliant ice compressing
spring's response
in crystal revelations that expand
as fasting will expand
the chastened heart.

1984.

Austerity: Its Grace in Time in Autumn

1.
The days retrench their luxuries of light. Soon
crisp-rayed chrysanthemums
chilled by light's withdrawal
will bend limp heads gradually
to a succession of freezing points.

The heart's grave wisdom craves this austerity:
intimate, evanescent things beloved
brought to this pathos:
friend, home, animal, garden, vulnerable
to time's privations, changes, darkness, silence,
distance, absence, cold.

Realities that evoke reverence, tenderness
show the heart its deepest truth:
its helplessness.

2.
Earth's fall obituaries list the same
loved things spring inventories name: the rose.
The rose lies dead
under a mausoleum of old leaves
dry brown and still as stone. The name
of dahlia, poppy, marigold—each raise
a brilliant memory. Petunia, a darkly fragrant bruise.
Violet, pansy, daisy, mignonette—their epitaph:

"These dared the pathos of their flowering." And we?

We know the human sadness, kin to joy
in what we never were and cannot be.
It draws us, finite, to infinity.

1984.

96

For the Returning Ones

"... All things fall and are built again ..." W.B. Yeats

I watch a late somerfest on the lawn.
Formations, choruses, flights
express what needs to be expressed
before migrations: routes, stop-overs, seeds,
berries, water, heights ... all
the rules and regulations.
                                    Leafless dark boughs
reveal the weathered nests where
scores of nostalgic calls
fall on the air, bracing as frost.

I'm house-cleaning.
Against ash or oak tree
I shake a dusty potpourri from my broom
and see my fallen hair, gray-brown as autumn
float with the dust into matted grass,
maple and arbor vitae.

Listless in the wind the long thin
strands of my hair loop themselves
into nature's loom, a new pattern, my gift
for spring-time weavers,
those mating, nesting, singing,
returning ones.

1984.

Is

I know in my bones that "'is" alone is never lost
in the zones of time. Being God's verb, "is" welds
ephemeral with eternal, expressing the nature of love,
the movement of angels.

Whether sad or at peace I know in my heart that "is," accepted,
pays reverence to reality, is ever confirming
all of creation in its own presence. Its recognition is
like cheers at processions of wonders and heroes; is
like bowed heads and tears when a coffin is carried.

"Is" continuously stills for me the rush of impressions;
corrects and redeems imagination's errors, the senses' imprecisions;
brings the clear truth home to the puzzled heart;
pervades the spirit with peace in its sadness and pathos.

At one moment "is" may reveal that a hurricane's force
is hurling your home into the sea. Or it may be that a cell
in your body threatens your life's blood. Or that one
dearer than life to you is in sorrow. A catastrophe asks you
to let it all be because this smallest verb, "is"
is God's verb of freedom; is present and singular and speaks
in the third person where there is no "I," no ego; where
each object, person, occurrence, thing—think of it!—

takes this form of the verb "to be"
with its infinite kernel; its authority.

"Is" moves our sentences into frames of light and is
implicit in everything; is like a hummingbird feeding,
staying itself in time, winging in place. Reality
is there, and reveals that the prism
is breaking the sunlight. That the tune you sing
is the melody of the hymn. That the ginkgo tree
is hung with fan-like leaves and in autumn
is gold. That beneath the willows the path you follow
is thick with dead leaves. That beauty, in truth,
is love's reality and carries its changeless grace like an angel
through all that is. And "is"
accepts what is: the breaking and falling and clouding and dying;
the burning forest, the wounded eagle and elk. "Is"
keeps "should have" and "may be," moods
of relentless pathos
flowing with time, dynamic, inseparable from
earth's beauty and love.

1985.

99

As Anniversaries Go

"You must hallow the fiftieth year . . . proclaim liberty . . ." Leviticus

I take reference from my beginnings. In memory they retain
temporal heavens: a meadow
threaded with gentians. Those reverent presences:
clouds over an autumn field, the stubble of wheat
level with rose hips. The season folded,
its future within it.

Anniversaries, yours going golden, and mine, cause me
to pause over a stretch of time, my one
particular pilgrimage, a Providence. I trace
a company of presences who walk gently with me
in spirit, in jubilee. The grace of the living, of
the long absent ones, in love, throng round, extend hands
to bless us on these anniversaries.

An anniversary identifies the moment
the future is made present in the past where time
accelerates its withdrawal of our years, days, moments.
Life is full, is still. And I can't tell
whether space moves time along until I note
the temporal scene changing (as on a boat only the shoreline
moves) and the notices, posted, show
expectations of heaven that are miles ahead
or around the corner. There are the chrysanthemums, there
the sunflowers last glow. My timeless life and yours
expressed in these deaths bequeathing us
the golden-vested moment that transcended
what was of moment in my diaries. The moment begins
to lift me to unself consciousness, to liberty.
To vision.
What is of moment is present: deaths
pressing against time's limits constantly
loosening strands of my biography. All that we hallow
held in the frailest webs of memory—elsewhere,
in heaven held timeless, holy, dear, hallowing
this year, proclaiming this liberty.   1985.

100

Bread and Butter Note: For a Host of Blessings

After a winter visit
here is a letter, paper white, undated,
dropped overnight at your window.
Its fresh folds show asterisks. They indicate
brilliant footnotes in sparrow-prints, telling
how gently cared for she is, this small chirping one
who traced a precise map for miles in the snow to discover
something to feed upon, a largesse: hidden berries
in hedges, fruit under the winter trees, in gardens
from summer's autumn, the seeds to stoke her flight and song.

O you of more worth than many sparrows, this letter is yours.
Read in the glow of itself it reveals the day's events, guiding
like angels. This white letter is quiet, its eloquence low key.
See, even the gray squirrel sits up, folds its front paws
lightly upon its white chest, listening. The message is creation's
reverent joy in itself, my reverent joy in you.
Undated forever this letter's timeless mode is present in hope
deeply stirred, at peace with this pathos, this longing to collect
the scattered bygones of love's providence:
the spacious room given over, the gracious table spread,
a host of blessings tending to the guest.

1986.

Three Acts of Love

"To write the poem is an act of love."
Dorothy Sayers, *The Mind of the Maker*

1.   In the Meadow
We kept our distance, delicately near
as lovers in familiar reverence,
with eyes made holy, open as the hand
that lifts a sacred gift in sacrifice.

Such was the gesture of our bones and flesh
before the black-eyed-susan and the moth—
lest from the weight of our admiring gaze
we should unbalance with a heavy glance
the lovely dance of butterfly and weed,
the still mobility of autumn love
poised in the self-possession of all giving.

2.   In the Garden
Changing and changeless under mobile skies
in the recurring gardens of September
love still creates what we in hope remember:
chrysanthemums are brought to their perfection,
our shadows move toward noon in one direction,
the rose to earth, the earth to rose is given,
the seeds of time grow our continuous heaven
changeless and changing under mobile skies.

3.   Before the Sunflower

Our earth explains our God. Daphne's myth
told ancient Greeks something about Apollo
who made immobile movements of her flight
as proof that gods make fruitful yes or no.
She, his swift love, became the green-boughed
laurel.

The myth explaining us explains our God.
Within the daily round like the sunflower
we grow erect and taller than we are
corrected by His light the livelong day,
our motivation in His golden Face.

1986.

Memory Raises Its Halo

Memory raises its halo over a white house
at prairie crossroads. It's there always,
childhood's enfolding home. The contour of peace,
its essence, that gentleness, settles like mourning doves
along stripped boughs potentially green, inwardly timed
for each season.
Your house harbors now this pain of dissolution—
what ruin releases from earth and air: a birthplace
free of its temporal framework, lit with the subdued
pure brilliant light of disillusionment.
You face the temporal, watch it fade naturally
into its past as things do from day to day
like grass, like flowers swiftly or slowly blown
as the weather goes. You barely feel the heartache.
You've memory. Fields of hope uncultivated, unfenced.
Wild roses grow freely, spread themselves richly over those
faraway ditches once mown for their hay. Now the delicate
rose fragrance lightly rises, dispelling those scents
cultivated, dense, that wreathed too earnestly
the funerals.

No endings here. Just the natural way things happen.
Like autumn's upper sixties into frost, then leaf by leaf,
winter wheeling spring in, earth turning as it does
away from light and back again, snow into crocus, crocus into
rose. And who knows when this rest home will
open into a birthplace, the gentleness there, and all
the original love, the wonder.

1987.

A New Name

"I will give him a white stone with a new name written on it."

Revelations 2, 17

White, its definition: the solar spectrum
reflected (invisible) as from a drift of new snow.
Stone: a fragment of earth, its former bloom, its seasons,
its æons of life compressed: leaf, flower, flesh, bone.

The new name on the white stone. Given to you,
its calligraphy clear, each letter kneeling in light, spelling
in gold of charity, in lowly sienna, in aquamarine, azure,
with pure red from the rainbow's edge, true violet (patience).

You new name divines you: God's knowing, His calling.
Divines your responding, (unknowing) your tracing with grace
this new name, new on the white stone, its revelation whole,
harmonius, radiant, in love given.

1987.

Earth Cloud and Lasting City

Our city's obscured. It's all but lost
in this earth cloud, a still cloud. In its
wingless descent it frees
the longings we chant again and again in the psalm:

"out of the depth I cry . . . hear me . . ."

What can we say
having here
no lasting city.

Bereft of our bearings, our memories, we're left
without distances, direction.
We mourn the slow darkening
of light's revelations: our dwellings, gateways, a turn in the road;
familiar things: the fields and sheepfold.   And the homescapes:
the balcony tree, geraniums, sparrows. In each direction
horizons blur. Now
the earth clouds our everywhere, a holy reminder
of full and final forgetting. We're bound here to await
the time-lifting cloud-break,
the very heaven we enter
day after day in prayer

though the heights are curtained. Within the room
cloud-grey silvers the window glass until out there
it mirrors inside things: a sofa, books on shelves, books
piled high beside a chair. House violets, Norfolk pine
alive in clay pots. Under the cloud-shadow all these become
ghosts of themselves, borne up, hovering purple, white, rose,
(centered golden), green. Their spirits float free over opaque
spaces: table, shelves, floor. Their reflections foretell
with *esprit* the endless glow of the world's goodness—hints
of a lasting city.

A lasting city. There. The wholeness of good.
Its dearness. Its expression waits until the vision,
the very word for it fills
syllable by syllable on the tongue, pure from the heart's intent,
shapes
that single Word, unclouded. Its recognition true. We're
styled to that deep regard. The word for love
undiminished by exaggeration.
Without possessive or superlative: the Good
incomparable and shared.
Our lasting city.

1988.

Tuition

Bone is left to pay to earth
the simple fee the body owes
for earth's curriculum of air;
its breathing greens; its apples trees;
the crystal subtleties it throws
into the snowdrifts that presage
a growing season for the rose;
for space where body learned to move—
to balance, float, reach outward, kneel;
for tide of minerals bone and blood
drew from earth's veins of ore, its seas,
to form the face, the hands that feel,
the nerves that link all life to these;
for light through which the searching eyes
transmit each image to the brain
where the unanswered Question lies
when bone at last shall pay in kind
tuition for each deep-drawn breath
of life so tutored; payment sealed
in bone's white enveloped, self-addressed
to earth at death

when soul, itself alive with grace,
its new name written on white stone,
finds all its debt by Love erased;
its Question answered in one Word;
its bones' reunion Life-insured;
its whole debt paid by Love alone.

1989.

Part 5
Poems of the 1990s

"We're evanescences eternalized in Spirit"
— from *Evanescence*, 1994

In the National Cemetery, Fort Snelling: For John

"They shall never again feel hunger or thirst, the sun shall not beat on them nor any scorching heat . . ." Revelations 7:16

Up the rugged slopes, over tiers of graves he carries
a trinity of white lilies. It's Easter-tide. He sees
among the numbered mounds a bunch of blooms set down
beside a veteran's stone. A living sign to everyone who comes.
Someone is still around who loves and mourns the one
whose bones lie here amid what seems
acres of lonely anonymity. Dust unto dust returning.
Spirits free. "Eye hath not seen, ear has not heard . . ." and yet
over the graves there's nothing but the sky. He ponder this.

He with the lilies is an only son and comes alone in search
of that identical white stone that bears his father's name
engraved like all the others with their dates
yet bare of ornament or epitaph. He finds the stone
and lays the lilies there and bows his head and prays
above the earth that holds his father's bones.

The boundless open space becomes for him a private place
where he can talk at ease with his old dad. Confide in him.
Tell him his troubles. Ask the help he needs. His filial trust
clears a calm passageway and here, in peace,
his father's spirit listens and draws near
to where his son, his longed-for son has come
in silence heeding what his heart will hear.

Time passes with its light. The son bends now
to rearrange the lilies. Then he turns,
descends the slopes through the dull tiers of graves
with lightened steps, his heavy burden eased, his grief assuaged,
his hopes rekindled as he heads for home.

1991.

Evanescence

The potted violets declare
with frail assurance that,
with care,
what's loved will be forever
where
you found it by a window near
an easy chair. And
ever after that just everywhere.

We're evanescences
eternalized
in Spirit though
the body dies
on earth, our star. And we remain
most eloquently who we are

living out our timeless prayer
that gathers every dear and fair
and fleeting treasure
everywhere
and stays them there
with all the finest webs of
memory's snare.

Successively the moments flow
continuously until they grow
into durations that
the mountains show
along with shooting stars and
melting snow
and all the flowering things that
                         come and go.

There's proof that evanescence spares
what's loved because it's good,
it's true. It's all Creation—me and you.
Its gleaning brings our aging to
the gathering we've come to know—and then
the ripe fulfillment of
our letting go.

                And that gives ground
When all we love is lost and found.

So evanescence sweeps our earth, our sky,
Continuously as we observe time fly
Through fleet durations
to that by and by: Eternity.

And time's Good-bye
is not the end.
You bend to me
and I ascend
in silence those three
worn steps up
into the departing bus
(a racing Greyhound its logo)
it soon will cause long miles
to flow
into the distance where I go
as evanescence plays its role
in shifting parts into their whole.

Those potted violets are a part
of this long musing. And by heart
I know the ending word for Word:
"Eye has not seen; ear has not heard."

                              1994.

St. Catherine's Wood:
Reflections on an Autumn Scene

We looked in wonder from southwestern slopes,
facing the wind, facing the guardian wood
where every shade and shape of leaf was moved
to catch our ears with murmurs, hold our gaze
with bronze, gold, crimson, russet leaves
the windswept boughs let fall
within our old and ravaged,
dear and criss-crossed wood. But here—
it's true—year after year
Progress brings need to dig and dump and plough
now here—now there—where ecosystems grew
fresh revelations of the Love we knew:
the bottle gentians, lupine, ferns and moss,
the owl and thrush, the moth and butterfly—
a myriad of those shy and gentle lives that must
thrive upon trust—all there on common ground
like you and me. Their lives a providence
of earth and sky and love and mystery.

Some trees are bent with burdens not their own.
Some stand tall and open as a prayer
that hasn't yet received its sure response. Their
dignity, their strength will come to life
through temporal loss. Their life's austerity in ways
like monks whose spirits thrive through Lenten days.

What if today from every compass point
the Angels of the Earth called out, "Do not impair
the sole protection of the ozone layer. Do not unsheathe
the sun's life-fostering rays; do not pollute
the vital air you breathe; your temporal light
that gives you such delight. Love meant all these to be,
with sheltering trees, the mainstays of your life."

What if an Angel called to all of us in time
a louder, more peremptory "Wait! O, do not harm
the land, the seas, the trees!" And then revealed
that God, our Love, will now make all things new:
our ravaged planet and polluted air,
our ruined ecosystems' ecospheres. The stones
that tell our old earth's history, the song-birds' bones.
All that we mourn for in our Guardian wood.

All of creation that He looked upon
and found so good.

1994.
Published in *Re-Vision*, a publication of the
Abigail Quigley McCarthy Center for Women,
The College of St. Catherine, Winter, 1995.

Heritage

Eternal love through temporal flows.
A Heritage descends and grows
roots that every spring renew
the gardens and each window-view
of trees and flower-bordered walks,
the Dew-Drop that reflects the sky,
the chapel and the woods nearby.
All beauty lifts the learning heart.
Professors, lectures, books impart
wisdom, knowledge, words of power-
bearing truth, the spirit's flower.
Peace, joy, learning, grow and flourish.
Timeless legacies will nourish
truth in freedom, joy that knows
eternal love through temporal flows.
The Heritage of Dante's Rose.

1995.

Acknowledgements
(arranged by date of first publication)

"Elegy," *Commonweal*, January 8, 1960, p. 419; and *Body of Time: Poems for This Incarnation*, Part 4, "Continuity," North Central Publishing Company, 1971.

"For Pere Teilhard de Chardin at my Father's Grave," *Commonweal*, January 22, 1960, p. 194; and *Body of Time: Poems for This Incarnation*, Part 4, "Continuity," North Central Publishing Company, 1971.

"[To Christ, Our Lord]: A Nun Remembers Her Bridal Day," *Commonweal*, April 19, 1963, p. 93.

"[Elegy] For An Ornithologist," *Sisters Today*, August, 1963; and *Body of Time: Poems for This Incarnation*, Part 4, "Continuity," North Central Publishing Company, 1971.

"Elegy for Sister Angele," *America*, October 19, 1963, p. 456.

"The Mind Is Its Own Shape," *America*, January 30, 1965, p. 165; and *Body of Time: Poems for This Incarnation*, Part 4, "Continuity," North Central Publishing Company, 1971.

"Plato: A Girl's Thought," *Commonweal*, March 5, 1965, p. 739.

"Three Acts of Love," *Commonweal*, November 26, 1965, p. 236.

"Light Parable I: For Robert," *America*, April 22, 1967, p. 587; and *Body of Time: Poems for This Incarnation*, Part 2, "The Process Time," North Central Publishing Company, 1971.

"Pomegranate Seeds on Christmas Morning," *America*, December 23-30, 1967, p. 29; and *Body of Time: Poems for This Incarnation*, Part 1 "Seeds in the Snow," North Central Publishing Company, 1971.

"Time Is a Bone in the Sun," *Commonweal*, January 12, 1968; and *Body of Time: Poems for This Incarnation*, Part 2, "The Process Time," North Central Publishing Company, 1971.

"Bronx Neighborhood," *Commonweal*, November 15, 1968, p. 256.

"Audubon's Hummingbird: Note for a History of Gratitude," *Commonweal*, August 19, 1969, p. 191; and *Body of Time: Poems for This Incarnation*, Part 3, "Time Being," North Central Publishing Company, 1971.

"Nun with Young Girls in an Art Gallery," *Commonweal*, January 10, 1969, p. 469; and *Body of Time*, 1971, Part 3 "Time Being" North Central Publishing Company, 1971.

"The First Thaw," *Commonweal*, January 15, 1971, p. 370.

"Fireflies: A Poem for William of Ghana," (first stanza), *Commonweal*, April 2, 1971, p, 87; "A Poem of Cold Fires for William of Ghana," stanzas 1 and 2, *Body of Time, Poems for This Incarnation*, Part 1; "Seeds in the Snow," North Central Publishing Company, 1971.

"[Where] the Sun Lifts," *Body of Time: Poems for This Incarnation*, Part 1 "Seeds in the Snow," North Central Publishing Company, 1971.

"Reflections on a Library Window," *Body of Time: Poems for This Incarnation*, Part 2. "The Process Time," North Central Publishing Company, 1971.

"Time Is a Bone in the Sun," *Body of Time: Poems for This Incarnation*, Part 2, "The Process Time," North Central Publishing Company, 1971.

"If Space Is the Body of Time," *Body of Time: Poems for This Incarnation*, Part 2 "The Process Time," North Central Publishing Company, 1971.

"The Stems of Flowers Are the Pillars of the World," *Body of Time: Poems for This Incarnation*, Part 3 "Time Being," North Central Publishing Company, 1971.

"Seventy-Two Ways of Receiving Light," *Body of Time: Poems for This Incarnation*, Part 3, "Time Being," North Central Publishing Company, 1971.

"Preference," *Commonweal*, June 20, 1975, p. 205.

"Passage á la Poe," in *Program for the Opera*, "The Voyage of Edgar Allan Poe," by Dominick Argento, performed in St. Paul, Minnesota, April 24, 1976, North Central Publishing Company.

"Lines from a Primitive," *Commonweal*, March 4, 1977, p. 135.

"Watching the Olympics," *Commonweal*, August 5, 1977, p. 504.

"Snowdrift," *Commonweal*, July 21, 1978. p. 455.

"Saint Catherine's Wood: Reflections on an Autumn Scene," *Revision*, a publication of the Abigail Quigley McCarthy Center for Women, The College of St. Catherine, Winter, 1995.